TALES FROM THE GREEK MYTHS

I Am the Goddess Aphrodite

Kostas Poulos
Illustrated by Sofia Papadopoulou

Translated by Leo Kalovyrnas

metaichmio

1st edition April 2018

ORIGINAL TITLE Κώστας Πούλος,
Είμαι η Αφροδίτη, Μεταίχμιο 2018

TRANSLATED FROM THE GREEK LANGUAGE BY Leo Kalovyrnas
ILLUSTRATED BY Sofia Papadopoulou

ISBN 978-618-03-1452-6
AUXIL. COMPU. CODE 81452
C.E.P. 4328 C.P. 9745

© 2017 METAICHMIO Publications
and Kostas Poulos

Bookstores
1. 18 ASKLIPIOU STR., 106 80 ATHENS
TEL. +30 210 3647433, FAX: +30 211 3003562
Internet Site: www.metaixmio.gr
e-mail: metaixmio@metaixmio.gr

2. POLYCHOROS, 118 IPPOKRATOUS STR., 114 72 ATHENS
TEL. +30 210 3003580, FAX: +30 211 3003581

For little Aphrodite Piechota
K.P.

I am astoundingly beautiful. Everyone who lays eyes on me cannot help but exclaim that I'm divine. And they are right, for I'm Aphrodite, the goddess of beauty.

My parents are Zeus and Dioni. I was born out of the sea off the shore of Kithira island. I sprang forth from the froth of the waves. I travelled the high seas for many days on top of a conch shell, until the wind carried me all the way to the shores of Cyprus. There I was met by the three Hours with their strange-sounding names: Thallo, Auxo, and Carpo. They were delighted to make my acquaintance.

'What are you doing on this island?' I asked them.

'We help plants grow and bear fruit,' Thallo replied, for indeed that was their job.

I remained in Cyprus in the company of the Hours and had a great time. They taught me a lot: about the four seasons, the rain, and warm and cold weather. They also gave me a golden belt to wear and be admired by everyone. With this belt around my waist I travelled to the top of Mount Olympus, where the other gods proclaimed me goddess of beauty and love.

I was tasked with making people fall in love. Not just mere mortals but gods, too. I always keep a little winged deity by my side; his name is Eros, but he's better known as Cupid. Cupid flies about with his bow and arrow. Now and then, I tell him to shoot his arrows at two people, and the moment they get wounded by his arrows, they fall madly

in love. It's really funny watching people in love. Sometimes they behave so foolishly, smiling stupidly for no reason at all, finding it hard to fall asleep, and becoming terribly absent-minded. If you ask them what the time is, they are likely to reply, 'Fine, thank you.'

A lot of gods wanted me as their wife. My father Zeus was wise enough to know that this might lead to terrible feuds and quarrels, so he married me off as soon as possible.

'You should take Hephaestus for a husband,' he told me. 'He's a really kind, hardworking, loving god, with a rare gift for honesty.'

You should have seen the parties we used to throw on Mount Olympus! They were simply divine! We ate ambrosia, and drank nectar, we told lots of jokes, but sometimes we quarrelled too. Usually our fights were caused by Eris, a nasty little deity whose name means Strife. That's why Zeus stopped inviting her to our parties. Even so, one day she gate-crashed a feast we were having. For a brief moment she stood at the door, but as soon as she saw Zeus staring angrily at her, she ran off, but only after she had tossed an apple in the middle of the hall. Now this apple was golden and had an inscription on it: "For the most beautiful one". At once I made a go for it, but so did Athena and Hera, who wanted it for themselves.

'I'm the most beautiful one,' said Athena.

'Fat chance! I am!' said Hera.

'Please, ladies!' I said. 'Everyone knows there is only one goddess of beauty that is me, Aphrodite.'

This would have ended in a serious brawl had it not been for Zeus, who intervened and managed to separate us.

'Stop all of you!' he shouted. 'What will mortals think if we gods behave as pettily as they do? Calm yourselves down, and we'll find a solution.'

True enough, the father of all gods and mortals came up with one. Saying that he was both unable and unwilling to choose objectively who the most beautiful goddess was, he decided to appoint another judge, a young prince by the name of Paris, the son of Priam, the king of Troy. Since it wasn't proper for Paris to be invited to Olympus, we three goddesses went to find him on a mountain near Troy, where he was tending his sheep – princes were often shepherds back then.

We stood before him and waited for quite a long time for him to reach a decision. It was clear that he was finding it really hard to choose who the fairest of all was. So Hera told him:

'If you give the apple to me, with the help of my husband Zeus I'll make you a great king.'

Athena looked daggers at Hera, and spoke up, 'If you give it to me, however, I'll turn you into a wise and brave warrior.'

Paris then turned and looked at me, the last one.

'If I am given the apple, I'll tell Cupid to shoot his arrow at the fairest woman in the entire world and make her fall in love with you.'

Paris remained thoughtful for a moment and then gave the apple to the fairest of them all, which was me of course! The other two goddesses looked at him with great resentment.

I, on the other hand, was extremely happy. And I kept my promise. When sometime later Paris was on a visit at Menelaos's palace in Sparta, I sent Cupid to strike the Fair Helen with his arrow and fill her heart with love for the handsome stranger. Sadly, that love brought on a lot of grief and destruction. It caused a war to break out, the Trojan War, that lasted a long ten years.

Everyone said that Hephaestus was the ugliest Olympian god, but he didn't seem so ugly to me. Granted, there were more handsome gods on Olympus. Take Ares, for example, the god of war. At first, Hephaestus and I were having a great time together, because he was really honest and hardworking, the best craftsman that ever was. He battled with fire and iron in his smithy and on most days came home late, feeling

very tired. So one afternoon as I was sitting at home all alone with nothing to do, Ares happened to pass outside my window. I stepped outside just to say hi.

'Hello,' I said.

'Hi there,' he greeted me back.

And it was at that moment that little Cupid got the chance to shoot us both with his arrows.

From that day onward, I found it hard to sleep and was constantly absent-minded. Whenever Hephaestus asked me what time it was, I just replied, 'Fine, thank you'. My behaviour made him suspicious, so he came up with a plan: he crafted a very fine iron net. So one day, when Ares dropped by and I offered him something to drink, this net fell from the ceiling on top of us, trapping us both so tightly that we were unable to move. Hephaestus came out of his hiding place and called all the other gods to see and make laughing stocks of us. Obviously I was not happy at all about any of this, so after that I avoided Olympus and spent most of my time in Cyprus.

I also travelled to lots of other places making people fall in love. I liked to see them so happy, wanting to move in together, have children and grandchildren. I also saw quite a few people getting married without being in love and I felt sorry for them. I told Cupid to strike them with his love arrows, but there are so many people in the world, and no matter how hard I try, I can't make everyone fall in love.

I am still worshipped and respected to this day. I exist practically everywhere. You can see me in almost every museum. In recent years, I like hanging out at the Louvre Museum in Paris. People from around the world flock there to admire me, well not me exactly, but a statue of me. It was crafted by a great sculptor. Obviously no mortal can ever know what a goddess looks like, but I think that that particular one came pretty close. I usually go to the museum on holidays, when it's closed, and I just sit there admiring my statue. I am made of marble from the island of Paros, which is unlike any other. It glows with an uncanny light, the light of the Aegean Sea, and it shows me as I really am: dazzlingly gorgeous! I am the Aphrodite of Milos.

I am not one to brag, but I am absolutely gorgeous. Simply divine!

LET'S LEARN ABOUT... THE GODDESS APHRODITE

The ancient Greeks worshipped dozens of gods and goddesses: not just the twelve Olympian deities but lots of other deities that were chiefly regional, which means that they were worshipped only in specific parts of the country. The most prominent ones in the religion of **all ancient Greeks**, however, were the **twelve Olympians**.

Aphrodite, the goddess of love and beauty, was the daughter of Zeus and Dioni, whose father was either the Sky or the Ocean. There's another version to this story, according to which Aphrodite rose out of the foam of the sea that frothed when bits of the Sky's flesh fell in, after his son, Cronus, had chopped them off. The wind carried the young goddess to Kithira and then to Cyprus, whereupon she came ashore on Pafos beach. According to another version of the myth, Aphrodite rose out of the waves already in Pafos, where she was welcomed by the three Hours, who then escorted her to Olympus. Aphrodite was waited upon not only by the three Hours, but also by the three Graces, and of course the winged Cupid, who was her son according to some myths.

Zeus had her marry Hephaestus, the god of fire and metalworking, but the beautiful goddess of love had a lot of other lovers, such as the god Ares, and the mortals Anchises and Adonis.

Aphrodite was able to make even gods fall in love with mere mortals. She inspired romantic love in people, helped those in love and protected marriage. Her two main places of worship were in Pafos, Cyprus, and Kithira, Greece. However, there were a lot of other holy sites dedicated to her, as for example in Sparta, where she was called Areia, meaning 'warlike', because she was worshipped as a warrior goddess due to her connection with Ares. In Knidos, a city in Minor Asia, she was called Euploia, which means she who ensures ships travel safely – after all, she was born out of the sea.

There were several symbols and animals associated with Aphrodite, such as myrtle, doves, sparrows, horses, and swans.

CROSSWORD

1. The name of the winged god that accompanied Aphrodite.
2. Aphrodite's mother
3. One of the three Hours.
4. An important temple to Aphrodite was located on this island.
5. Aphrodite's husband.

ANSWERS: 1. CUPID, 2. DIONI, 3. CARPO, 4. CYPRUS, 5. HEPHAESTUS

▶ The vase above shows Aphrodite. Take a close look at the image and answer the following questions:

- How is the goddess portrayed?
- What is she holding?
- Which symbols of hers do you recognize?
- Where might she be going?

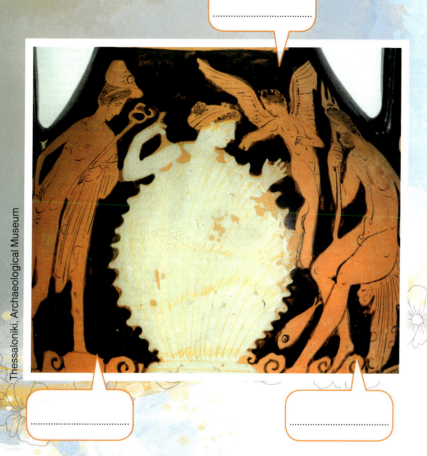

▶ The image above is from an ancient vase, and shows the birth of the goddess of beauty.

- Which version of the myth has the artist chosen to portray?
- Can you name the gods that are watching? Write down their names. (Tip: notice what they are holding to find who they are.)

▸ Nowadays, there are no goddesses of beauty and love, but we have lots of beautiful movie stars and show-business celebrities whom we worship for their beauty. Which male or female stars do you admire for their beauty?

▸ Beauty is in the eye of the beholder, as the saying goes. What do you think makes a person beautiful? Is it just their physical appearance? Or can it also be their personalities, sense of humour, kindness, etc? Make a list of what makes a person beautiful for you.

- Read the following information, use some of the myth versions already given, or come up with a version of your own to complete and paint the statue of Aphrodite below.

The most famous statue of the goddess of beauty that still survives to this day is **Aphrodite of Milos**, better known as Venus de Milo. It dates back to 100 BC (Hellenistic era) and it's made of Paros marble. When it was discovered both arms were missing. Perhaps Aphrodite held an apple or a mirror in her left hand, or Ares's shield with both hands. According to others, the goddess wasn't holding anything but was preparing to wash her hair.

Sofia Papadopoulou

Sofia Papadopoulou lives and works in Athens, Greece. She studied Architecture at the National Technical University of Athens. After completing her studies, she began working professionally on children's book illustrations. She has worked with publishers such as Metaichmio, Kedros, Psichogios and Ocelotos. For the illustration of the book I'm telling you I'm not a monster, Kedros 2011, she was nominated for DIAVAZO magazine's awards. In January 2013 she exhibited her works as a solo artist in the 'Laspi Workshop' and has participated in various festivals. She was a student of the painter and sculptor Vasilis Katsivelakis, and is now being tutored by painter Pavlos Nikolakopoulos. Alongside her artistic work, she is a technical drawing instructor, preparing students for entering architectural and design faculties.

Kostas Poulos

Kostas Poulos was born in Elikonas, Viotia. He studied philology at the Universities of Athens, Würzburg, and Munich, and worked as a secondary school teacher both in Greece and abroad. He has written, translated and adapted several books for adults but chiefly for children for many publishing houses (Livanis, Boukoumanis, To Rodakio, Papadopoulos, Metaichmio). Some of his most famous books include: *Sun in the Garden*, *Half A Chocolate Is A Joke*, *One Ice-Cream Lasts Too Little*, *Nikos And The Wolf*, *Theofilos The Painter*, *Maria Callas*, *Scheherazade*, etc. His series of children's books The Greek Ones (Papadopoulos Publishers) includes classical texts of Greek literature from Homer to the present day especially adapted for kids. Poulos has also worked as a reader, editor, and reviewer for magazines and newspapers. His work has been translated into other languages and adapted for the theatre.

TALES FROM THE GREEK MYTHS
SERIES

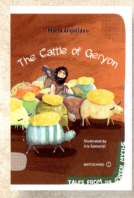

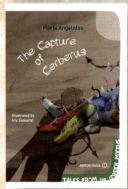

www.metaixmio.gr

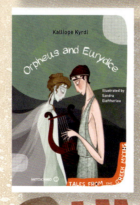

9786180314526.2

Educational material included

I am Aphrodite, the goddess of beauty and love. No other woman, mortal or divine, surpasses me in beauty. Hera and Athena once took it in their heads that they were fairer than me, but a handsome young fellow by the name of Paris judged us all and gave me the first prize – a golden apple.

This series offers a new reading of the ancient Greek myths. They are not old, worn-out stories, but gripping tales of timeless human adventures, containing all the fears and joys that have marked and continue to mark the human soul.

ISBN: 978-618-03-1452-6

9 786180 314526

AUXIL. COMPU. CODE 81452

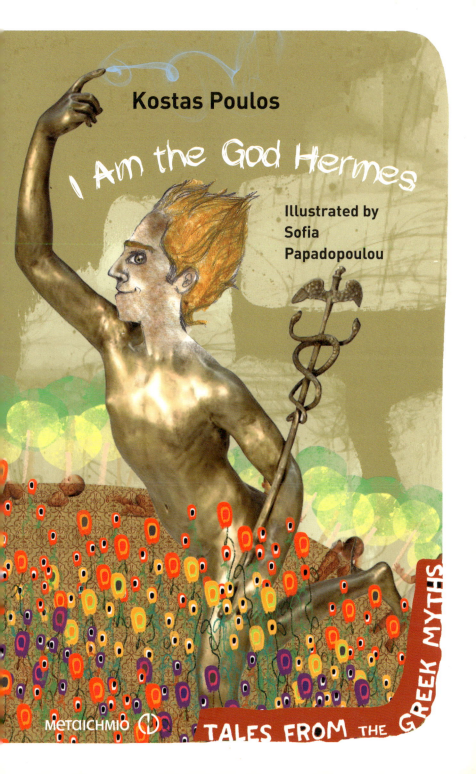